W0082290

Within Our Power

The Story of the Edenton Ladies' Tea Party

Rebecca Bondfield

Sarah Littlejohn

Penelope Bark

© 2024 by the North Carolina Office of Archives and History
All rights reserved.

978-0-8652-6506-6

D. Reid Wilson
Secretary, North Carolina Department of Natural and Cultural Resources

Dr. Darin J. Waters
Deputy Secretary, North Carolina Office of Archives and History

Ramona Bartos
Director, North Carolina Division of Historical Resources

Ansley Herring Wegner
Research Supervisor

Sheilah Barrett Carroll
Book Designer

2024 NORTH CAROLINA HISTORICAL COMMISSION

David Ruffin
CHAIR

The Honorable Newell Clark
Shana Bushyhead Condill
Dr. David Dennard
Samuel B. Dixon
Barbara Groome
Dr. Valerie A. Johnson
Dr. Susanna M. Lee
Susan Phillips
W. Noah Reynolds
Barbara B. Snowden
EMERITI: Kemp P. Burpeau, Mary Lynn Bryan, Alan D. Watson

Within Our Power was set in Adobe Caslon, Estonia, Franklin Gothic,
P22 1722 Pro, and P22 Franklin Caslon.

Distributed by the University of North Carolina Press

Printed in Canada

For all who bravely use their voice to speak truth to power.
Sally

For my sisters, Heather, Danielle, and Kristin,
who are all amazing and strong.
John

EDENTON, CHOWAN COUNTY
The Colony of North Carolina

❧ Summer 1774 ❧

Penelope Barker passed a tea cup to her friend Jean Blair. The tea had a slightly smoky taste with just a hint of cinnamon. It perfectly suited the ladies' discussions, no matter what the topic.

Penelope and Jean drank tea in the morning, the afternoon,
and in the evening. Friends and relatives often joined them.
While they sipped tea, they spoke about many things.

During 1774, they talked a lot about unfair treatment.

1

At that time, the country called Great Britain had many
colonies in North America. A colony is a land that is ruled by
another country. North Carolina, where Penelope and Jean lived,
was a colony. Many people who lived in the North American
colonies called themselves Americans. But Britain's King George III
was still their ruler.

Two groups of men, called Parliament, helped King George make Great Britain's laws. (Women could not be members of Parliament. They did not have that power.) The men in Parliament came from all areas of Great Britain. Wealthy men from each area chose a man to be their representative in Parliament. He was their voice. He told other members of Parliament and the king what the people in his area wanted and needed.

The American colonies did not have a representative in Parliament. People in America had no voice. Penelope, Jean, and their fellow Americans did not think that was fair.

They thought something else was unfair.

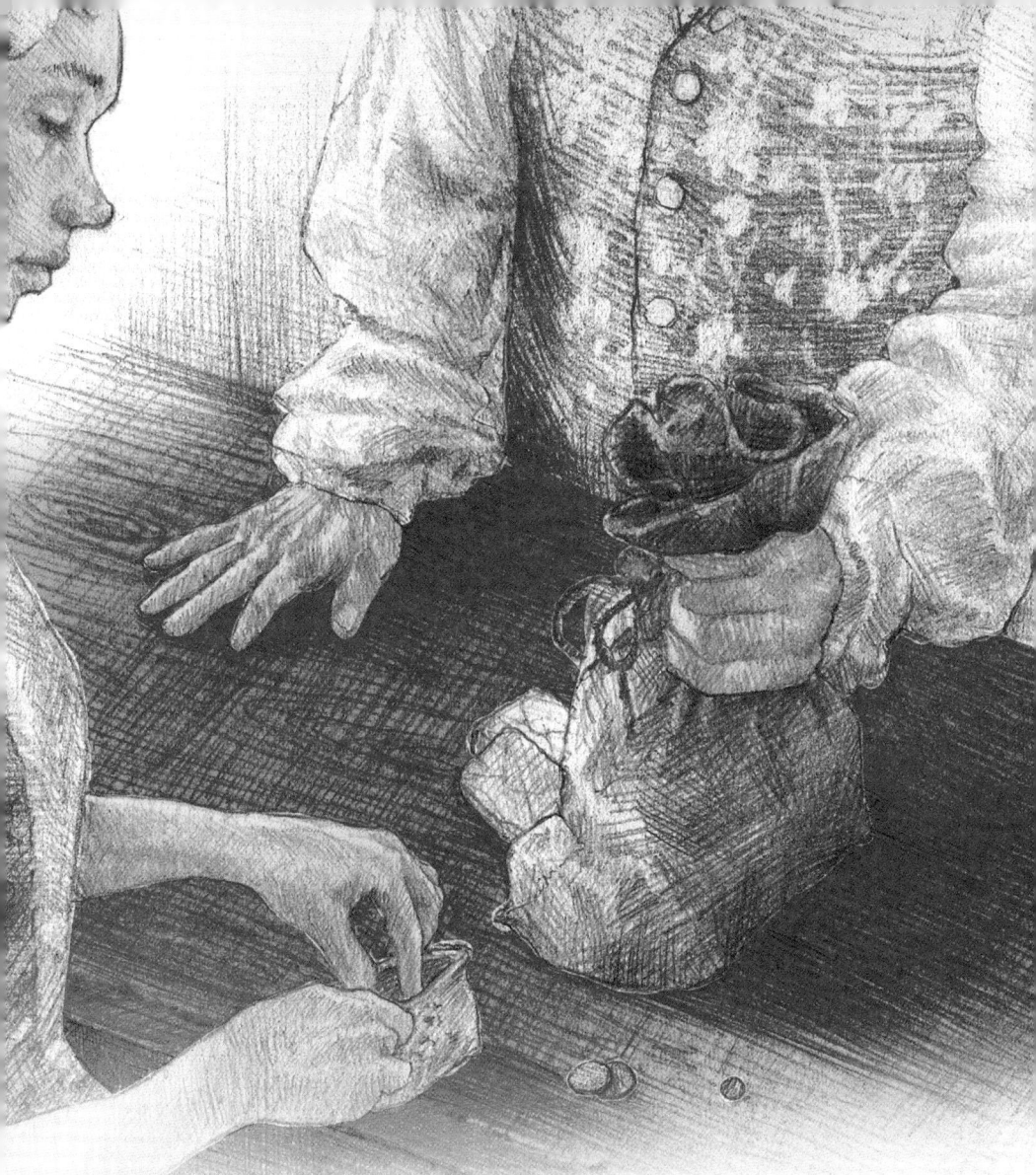

Great Britain's laws guaranteed certain rights to all British subjects. People had the right to own property, such as a home, clothing, horses, cows, furniture, books. They had the right to keep the money that they earned. In return, they gave some of their earnings to the British government. This money, called taxes, was used to help run Great Britain and its colonies. People who owned land paid taxes on it. Taxes were part of the price that people paid when they bought items.

British subjects who lived in Great Britain had a voice in how tax monies were spent. This was not true in the American colonies.

Parliament made laws that said Americans had to pay taxes on items shipped to the colonies from other places. These included popular goods such as paper, sugar, and especially tea.

But Americans had no representative in Parliament. Without one, they had no voice to tell the government how their tax money should be spent. Americans said that was "taxation without representation."

Penelope, Jean, and their fellow Americans *definitely* did not think *that* was fair. It made them angry.

People on horseback and in boats brought newspapers from other places to Edenton. *The Virginia Gazette* was a popular one. When these papers arrived, Edenton neighbors shared the information they contained.

A year earlier, in 1773, Edenton residents read news that Parliament made a new law. It allowed one company—the East India Company—to bring tea directly to America. The East India Company did not pay a tea tax to Great Britain when it did this.

But when Americans bought the tea, they still had to pay the tax.
And the tax money they paid went to the British government.
Many Americans complained that was unfair! Without a voice in
Parliament, the Americans had not agreed to paying a tea tax.
It was taxation without representation!

The night of December 16, 1773, about 100 men in Boston, Massachusetts took action against the new law. They knew that three ships loaded with hundreds of chests of tea were anchored in Boston's harbor. To avoid being recognized, they rubbed their faces with coal dust. They carried hatchets and draped blankets across their shoulders. They chose items similar to those used by the Mohawk and Narragansett Indians.

The men climbed on board the ships, chopped open the tea chests, and threw them into the harbor. Ruined tea floated everywhere. People called this event the Boston Tea Party—but no one sat around and drank tea!

In response, the government declared no ships could enter or leave the harbor until the tea was paid for.

And then Parliament sent hundreds of soldiers to Boston to make sure it didn't happen again.

In the months after the Boston Tea Party, newspapers spread more news about Parliament's unfair treatment of Americans. Edenton's ladies didn't only learn about these events while sipping tea in their homes or by reading newspapers. People talked about it everywhere.

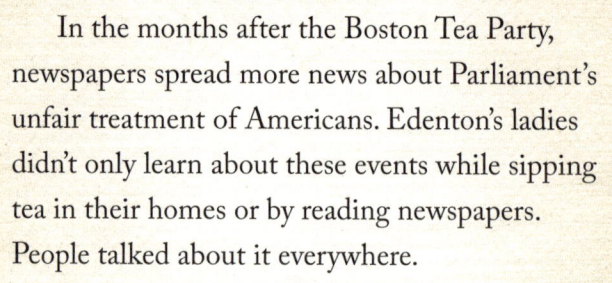

Abigail and Jasper Charlton probably discussed unfair taxation when they drank tea with their friends Frances and Samuel Johnston. Jasper and Samuel were well-known Edenton lawyers who often shared afternoon tea.

When Lydia Bennet visited her husband's shop, she may have added comments to conversations about taxation without representation while men bought new hats.

Sarah Littlejohn would not have been surprised if customers spoke about taxes while they purchased items in her husband William's dry goods store.

She definitely agreed that the tax on tea was unfair.

Anne Horniblow certainly heard heated discussions about it in the King's Arms Tavern, her family's inn.

Mary Hunter likely spoke about taxation without representation with her husband, Thomas. He and other men were already discussing what to do about unfair laws.

Penelope Dawson may have heard people complaining that they were not being treated as British subjects as she walked from the harbor to her cousin Jean Blair's house.

Penelope Barker probably mentioned how she and Edenton's residents felt about taxes in the letters that she sent to her husband. He had been living, for many years, in London, England, where he worked on North Carolina's behalf.

The men and women who lived in and near Edenton grew angrier and angrier about unfair treatment. Talking wasn't enough. They had to *do* something.

The morning of August 22, 1774, people bustled along King Street, heading toward the Chowan County courthouse. Men, such as Jean Blair's brother Samuel Johnston and Sarah Littlejohn's husband, William, were among those on the way to a meeting at the courthouse. The purpose of the meeting was to decide what to do about unfair laws and taxes.

Many Edenton women, including Penelope, Jean, and Frances Johnston were as angry as the men attending the meeting. Perhaps they wanted a voice in the decisions that were being made. But women were not allowed to be part of the government. They did not have that power.

Edenton's residents agreed to send representatives to an even bigger meeting. That meeting, called North Carolina's First Provincial Assembly, was scheduled for later that week in New Bern, the colony's capital city.

Representatives from all parts of North Carolina would be present and decide what the colony planned to do about unfair laws and taxes.

Frances Johnston and Mary Hunter's husbands, Samuel and Thomas, were two of the six men chosen to represent Chowan County in the Assembly.

In the days after the New Bern meeting, news spread about the Assembly's decisions.

North Carolinians agreed that they were loyal subjects to King George. They agreed that Americans were not being treated fairly, as Great Britain's system of laws had promised.

North Carolinians agreed that taxation without representation was unfair.

They considered a number of ways they would protest Great Britain's unfair treatment. One of the ways was to boycott (stop buying) goods that came from Great Britain or its colonies elsewhere. That included cloth. And tea.

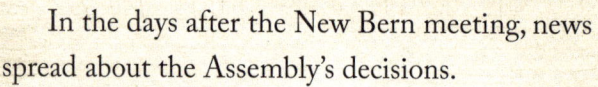

Penelope Barker and Jean Blair read letters printed in *The Virginia Gazette*. Some of them were written by women who lived in other American colonies. They urged the ladies where they lived to boycott British goods. Their letters were always signed anonymously, with names such as *"A Planter's Wife."*

Penelope, Jean, Abigail, Frances and their friends did not have the power to make decisions in the Assembly. But they had the power of something else: their names.

Together, they and their friends wrote a statement that declared *". . . it is a Duty which we owe, not only to our near and dear Connections . . . but to ourselves . . . to do every Thing as far as lies in our Power"* to support the declarations and resolutions made by the Assembly. That included boycotting tea. Instead, they would brew hot drinks from the plants that grew in the Americas.

Then they signed their names at the bottom of their declaration—something no other women had done. By October 25, 1774, fifty-one women had signed.

They sent their declaration to *The Virginia Gazette*. It was printed in the *Gazette* on November 3, 1774, and included all of their names. Fifty-one women from the Edenton area used their power and their voice to let their fellow Americans know exactly what they believed.

But it didn't end there . . .

Rebecca Bondfield

Sarah Littlejohn

Penelope Bark

On October 27, 1774, someone, perhaps Penelope Barker, sent a letter to London, England. It was addressed to the newspaper, *The Morning Chronicle and London Advertiser*. The writer enclosed a copy of the Edenton ladies' declaration. In the letter, the writer stated that the ladies of North Carolina publicly supported the Assembly's resolutions to boycott tea and not wear British cloth. The writer suggested that the newspaper publish the ladies' declaration. It would let British women know that American men *and* women were in agreement about Great Britain's unfair treatment.

The declaration and the names of its fifty-one signers appeared in the *Morning Chronicle* on January 16, 1775.

The Edenton ladies' declaration definitely caught the eye of many British women and men. Maybe it even reached the eyes of some members of Parliament. It showed everyone that the Edenton ladies were unafraid to use the power of their names to claim for themselves a public voice, one that called attention to their beliefs.

Their example shows how people can join together and create a strong voice that stands firm against injustice.

EDENTON, NORTH CAROLINA, *October* 25, 1774.

AS we cannot be indifferent on any Occasion that appears nearly to affect the Peace and Happiness of our Country, and as it has been thought necessary, for the publick Good, to enter into several particular Resolves, by a Meeting of Members deputed from the whole Province, it is a Duty which we owe, not only to our near and dear Connections, who have concurred in them, but to ourselves, who are essentially interested in their Welfare, to do every Thing as far as lies in our Power to testify our sincere Adherence to the same; and we do therefore accordingly subscribe this Paper, as a Witness of our fixed Intention and solemn Determination to do so.

ABIGAIL CHARLTON.	MARY BLOUNT.
F. JOHNSTON.	ELIZABETH CREACY.
MARGARET CATHCART,	ELIZABETH PATTERSON.
ANNE JOHNSTON.	JANE WELLWOOD.
MARGARET PEARSON.	MARY WOOLARD.
PENELOPE DAWSON.	SARAH BEASLEY.
JEAN BLAIR.	SUSANNAH VAIL.
GRACE CLAYTON.	ELIZABETH VAIL.
FRANCES HALL.	ELIZABETH VAIL.
MARY JONES.	MARY CREACY.
ANNE HALL.	MARY CREACY.
REBECCA BONDFIELD.	RUTH BENBURY.
SARAH LITTLEJOHN.	SARAH HOWCOTT.
PENELOPE BARKER.	SARAH HOSKINS.
ELIZABETH P. ORMOND.	MARY LITTLEDLE.
M. PAYNE.	SARAH VALENTINE.
ELIZABETH JOHNSTON.	ELIZABETH CRICKETT.
MARY BONNER.	ELIZABETH GREEN.
LYDIA BONNER.	MARY RAMSAY.
SARAH HOWE.	ANNE HORNISLOW.
LYDIA BENNET.	MARY HUNTER.
MARION WELLS.	TERESIA CUNNINGHAM.
ANNE ANDERSON.	ELIZABETH ROBERTS.
SARAH MATTHEWS.	ELIZABETH ROBERTS.
ANNE HAUGHTON.	ELIZABETH ROBERTS.
ELIZABETH BEASLEY.	

The orginal article as it also appeared in
The Virginia Gazette on November 3, 1774.

*Courtesy of Special Collections, John D. Rockefeller Library,
Colonial Williamsburg Foundation, Williamsburg, Virginia.*

❧ AUTHOR'S NOTE ❧

The Edenton Ladies' declaration was ground-breaking. Women were not expected to publish their opinions in a newspaper read by thousands of people. And certainly not in a declaration that included their names! Yet the Edenton ladies dared to speak.

Even though the Edenton women had no official voice in the colonial governments, they and many American women supported independence from Great Britain when war was declared.

According to oral tradition, Amelia, an enslaved woman in Penelope Barker's household, was present when some of the ladies signed the declaration. But then, women of African heritage had no official voice. Had Amelia been able to write, she would not have been asked to sign.

People of African and American Indian heritage could not serve in the colonial governments. In fact, the majority of them had few legal rights. Yet some free and enslaved Black men enlisted in the Continental Army or state militias and fought for independence.

In 1787, five years after the Revolutionary War ended, a group of White male delegates from the newly formed American states wrote a document called the Constitution of the United States. A year later,

it officially became the basis for how the nation's government would be run. But some things remained unfair. Even though they had no vote, women and people of African and American Indian heritage still had to pay taxes—without a voice in the laws that were passed to govern them.

It was a long time before the Constitution was changed to make the United States fair for most of its people. It completely abolished slavery in 1865. Black men became eligible to vote in 1870. In 1920 women were able to vote nationally. And in 1924, Native Americans were finally recognized as citizens of the United States. Only then were they nationally eligible to vote. Even today, many people face obstacles to voting and having their voices heard.

"Taxation without representation" was a rallying cry for colonial Americans. It was an early step toward creating a new government, one in which Americans used their voice to decide what was fair and what was not.

The Edenton Ladies' declaration showed the world that they were willing to sacrifice their comfort—even their safety— in the struggle for fair treatment. Their story is one of many that have combined to make the United States the nation that it is today.

North Carolina Timeline

12,000 years ago to present

Paleoindians and their descendants, which include the Catawba, Cherokee, Chowanoac, Meherrin, and Tuscarora, have lived in the region now called North Carolina for thousands of years.

1585

Roanoke Colony established by British colonists on Roanoke Island. Ultimately, the colony failed.

1712

The colony split into North Carolina and South Carolina.

1663

King Charles II of England granted a large area of land in North America to eight English men. The land was named the Province of Carolina, after King Charles I.

1776

April 12
North Carolina Provincial Congress instructs its delegates to the Continental Congress, in Philadelphia, to vote for independence from Great Britain.

July 4
The Declaration of Independence is adopted in Philadelphia, Pennsylvania. Joseph Hewes, John Penn, and William Hooper were the three North Carolinians who signed the Declaration. Hewes was from Edenton.

1783

Revolutionary War ends, Treaty of Paris.

1789

November 21
North Carolina becomes the 12th state in the Union.

1722
The city of Edenton was established as North Carolina's capital.

1729
The colony of North Carolina became a crown colony when seven of the men returned their rights to the land to Great Britain's King George II.

1766
New Bern becomes the colony's capital.

1774
August 25–27
Delegates from North Carolina counties meet in New Bern as the First Provincial Assembly.

October 25
Edenton Ladies write their declaration. Years later, it was called the Edenton Tea Party.

1773
December 16
Boston Tea Party.

1775
April 19
Revolutionary War begins in Lexington, Massachusetts.

Author and Illustrator Biographies

Sibert Medal winner Sally M. Walker (*Secrets of a Civil War Submarine*) is the author of more than 60 nonfiction books. *Sinking the Sultana* received Virginia's Jefferson Cup Award for history; *Written in Bone* was a YALSA Excellence in Nonfiction for Young Adults Award finalist. *Champion: the Comeback Tale of the American Chestnut* was an Orbis Pictus Honor Book. Walker's many other awards include ALA Notables, Orbis Pictus Honor Book, and NSTA Outstanding Science Trade Book. A number of her books have been finalists on the Master List for many states' Young Reader Awards.

Walker and Jonathan D. Voss previously collaborated on *Winnie: the True Story of the Bear that Inspired Winnie-the-Pooh*, which won Arizona's Grand Canyon Reader Award and New York's Charlotte Award.

I love art, music, and beautiful things. I've always been hugely inspired by others who bring this beauty to the world around us. Whether it's well crafted words in a book or a painting in a gallery, there is something stirring about it all.

I love the work of early illustrators like Arther Rackham, N. C. Wyeth, Howard Pyle, and Frank Schoonover. When I tell a story with pictures I want something to be felt. If an image falls flat, I haven't done my job well. When I illustrate a book, I approach it as though I'm moving a camera around the action. I get to decide where to freeze the frame. It's a big responsibility to tell a story well. I haven't figured it all out yet, but I'm loving the journey. Maybe one day, when I grow up, I'll be good at it. But, no matter where I end up, as I go, I hope that joy and pleasure are found in the words I write and the pictures I make.

If you'd like to know more about me and the work I do, visit me at www.jonathandvoss.com.